UNITED STATES
SUPREME COURT
LIBRARY

David Souter

by Bob Italia

Published by Abdo & Daughters, 6535 Cecilia Circle, Edina, Minnesota 55439.

Copyright © 1992 by Abdo Consulting Group, Inc., Pentagon Tower, P.O. Box 36036, Minneapolis, Minnesota 55435. International copyrights reserved in all countries. No part of this book may be reproduced in any form without written permission from the publisher. Printed in the United States.

Photo credits: AP/Wide World Photos-7, 9, 12, 16, 18, 35
                  Archive Photos-cover
                  UPI/Bettmann-4, 15, 26, 31, 32, 33, 37

Edited by: Paul Deegan

Library of Congress Cataloging-in-Publication Data

Italia, Robert, 1955-
        David Souter / written by Bob Italia ; [edited by Paul Deegan].
           p.   cm. — (Supreme court justices)
        Includes index.
        Summary: A career biography of Supreme Court Associate Justice David Souter.
        ISBN 1-56239-092-9
        1. Souter, David H., 1939-   —Juvenile literature. 2. Judges—United States—Biography—
Juvenile literature. [1. Souter, David H., 1939- . 2. Judges. 3. United States. Supreme
Court—Biography.] I. Deegan, Paul J., 1937- . II. Title. III. Series.
KF8745.S68I86 1992
347.73'2634—dc20
[B]
[347.3073534]
[B]
                                                                    92-13708
                                                                       CIP
                                                                        AC

Table of Contents

Not much was known about Justice David Souter when he joined the Supreme Court in 1990. He was a competent legal mind and lived privately and humbly in a small town in New Hampshire.

But since his appointment, Souter has provided the deciding vote on some of the more controversial issues of our day. If this pattern continues, the silent Yankee from New Hampshire may have a lot to say about how Americans may live their lives.

David Souter receives a kiss from his mother, Helen, after being sworn in as Supreme Court Justice.

Different than the Rest

David Hackett Souter was born in 1940. By the time he was eleven years old, his family moved to the tiny town of Weare, located in the outback of New Hampshire. There, Souter would remain for most of his life—except when he went away to school.

Souter attended Concord High School in New Hampshire. His classmates remember him as a shy and intelligent boy who always carried a leather briefcase.

Souter's high school yearbook picture.

"He was different from everybody else," said one classmate. "He may have found that painful but he wouldn't have shown it."

When he was a senior, Souter was president of the National Honor Society. He was also co-editor of the school yearbook, considered by many to be very sophisticated, and voted most likely to succeed.

David Hackett Souter

"Soutie"

xol

y 10,

12-

onal

Dra-

ppy

etic

Crimson Review 11, 12; National Honor Society 11, 12-pres.; Student Council 12; SYB-co-editor.

Very hard-working and studious — witty and in constant demand — enjoys "giving and attending scanda-

The caption under his yearbook photo read (jokingly): "Enjoys giving and attending scandalous parties."

After graduating from high school with honors, Souter enrolled in Harvard University in Cambridge, Massachusetts. There he studied philosophy. But his mind was already on law. Souter wrote his senior honor thesis on the aspects of Oliver Wendell Holmes' legal thought. Then he graduated magna cum laude.

Souter's efforts won him a highly-prized Rhodes Scholarship to Oxford University in London, England. Most Rhodes scholars use the opportunity to travel Europe. But Souter stayed put in London and studied.

Souter leaving church in New Hampshire.

Souter eventually returned to Harvard to attend its law school. He did well, though he failed to make the Law Review, an honor reserved for the best law students.

While in law school, Souter developed a charming personality. He even enjoyed smoking a cigar now and then.

"He was a fun and refreshing person," said a Harvard classmate. "He was a guy with a good glint in his eye."

After graduating from Harvard Law School, David Souter returned to New Hampshire and joined a private Concord law firm. But shortly after, the state's Attorney general's office in Concord lured him away from private practice. After eight years working as an assistant attorney general, David Souter became the attorney general himself.

While attorney general, Souter, a staunch Republican, was involved in some controversial matters that would impact his career. His defense of New Hampshire Governor Meldrim Thomson's attempt to fly the American flag at halfmast on Good Friday was unsuccessful. He also convicted protesters who demonstrated outside New Hampshire's Seabrook nuclear power plant.

Despite these controversial moves, Souter was a well-respected lawyer. His efforts were eventually rewarded when he was appointed as a New Hampshire Supreme Court judge.

The White House Calls

Souter spent seven years in the New Hampshire Supreme Court. He wrote over two hundred "opinions" (decisions) before he was named to the U.S. Court of Appeals in Boston, Massachusetts.

Three months later in July 1990, Souter received a call from C. Boyden Gray. Gray was President George Bush's legal counsel. He said President Bush wanted to see Souter in Washington, D.C. right away. U.S. Supreme Court Associate Justice William Brennan had just resigned, and President Bush was thinking of nominating Souter to replace Brennan.

Souter was stunned. He was used to a very orderly life. He hadn't even **A pleased and** unpacked all his books in **surprised Souter.** his office in Boston, and now he could very well be on the move again. But this was the opportunity of a lifetime.

Souter could not turn down the Republican president's request for an interview.

But after he hung up the phone, Souter remained stunned. He turned to a friend and said, "Why would the president want me?" He still could not believe what was happening.

Neither could President Bush. He was on the presidential airplane— Air Force One—when he got the news that Justice Brennan had decided to retire. Bush called Brennan and accepted his resignation. Then he called John Sununu, the White House chief of staff. He told Sununu to round up the names of possible candidates for the Supreme Court vacancy. A few days later, Bush had his wish list.

President George Bush (r) nominates Souter in 1990.

The swiftness with which the President moved to nominate a Supreme Court candidate caught many by surprise. But the White House had a good explanation.

"The President saw immediately that he needed to move quickly," said a White House official.

"Otherwise, the interest groups were going to take control of the debate, narrow his options and make confirmation more difficult."

The very next day following the telephone call from Gray, Souter found himself at the White House. **President George Bush (l) with Vice President Dan Quayle.** Presidential aides asked Souter many personal and difficult questions before he was allowed to see the president. They wantd to know if Souter had ever used drugs. He said no.

The presidential aides also wanted to know if Souter was a homosexual. (Souter was a 50-year-old bachelor who had lived with his mother most of his life.) Souter brushed aside the obvious bias and reassured the presidential aides that he was not a homosexual.

17

Finally, much to his relief, David Souter was allowed into the presidential study. He and President Bush enjoyed a much more enjoyable 40-minute discussion about Souter's qualifications. Afterward, Souter was escorted to the basement of the White House. There he awaited President Bush's decision.

Souter is sworn in before testifying at the Senate Judiciary Committee on Capitol Hill.

The Lady or the Yankee?

Bush was considering
another candidate as well. She was U.S.
Circuit Court Judge Edith Jones of Texas.
Jones also had many qualifications that
President Bush liked. She was a conservative
Republican. She was an opponent of abortion
rights—so too was President Bush.

There were some personal qualities Bush
liked about Jones as well. Jones was from
Bush's adopted state of Texas. Her parents
even had a home in Kennebunkport, Maine,
where Bush had a home. And she was a
woman who would earn Bush some points with
women's groups across the country.

Jones seemed like the better candidate of
the two. Even Vice President Dan Quayle
endorsed her. But United States Attorney
General Richard Thornburgh and presidential
counsel Gray fought hard for Souter. They
reminded the president that Souter was also a
conservative Republican who was even more
qualified: Harvard graduate, Rhodes scholar,
and a member of the U.S. Court of Appeals.

Even better, Souter was an unknown. It would be difficult to criticize Bush for his selection. And Souter was squeaky clean when it came to his private life. The Senate, who had to approve all Supreme Court nominees, would find no fault with Souter.

President Bush returned to the Oval office to ponder his choices. He wrote a memo on which he placed the strengths and weaknesses of each candidate. Finally, he made up his mind.

"I have pledged excellence," Bush wrote on the memo. "Souter is the most impressive here. I liked his manner—scholarly, serious approach, right age—temperment = A OK." David Souter, the Yankee from New Hampshire, was the President's choice for the U.S. Supreme Court.

Souter's nomination created a storm of controversy. The conservative Souter was replacing the Court's leading liberal justice. Many people feared the Court was becoming too conservative.

Conservatives and liberals alike wanted to know where Souter stood on the controversial subject of abortion. Conservatives and President Bush wanted the historic *Roe vs. Wade* case overturned. Those in favor of abortion wanted the ruling upheld.

Souter kept a typical low profile before the Senate confirmation hearings. He refused to tell anyone his views on abortion—or any other issue. He merely said that he would reply to the Senate questions with "constitutionally appropriate candor." Even President Bush said he did not know Souter's views on abortion.

"Neither side can find anything to support their pre-beliefs," said a White House aide, "so they're all nervous."

The Invasion of Concord

Both the conservatives and the liberals decided to find out all they could about Souter. Suddenly, the city of Concord, New Hampshire, found itself flooded with FBI investigators, Senate aides, and journalists. They were all looking for every written legal opinion David Souter had ever written.

They swarmed over records of the state courts, attorney general's office, and local papers, hoping to find some evidence of Souter's personal outlooks and philosophies. "We haven't had this much attention in years," said a Concord public librarian.

In court papers, the researchers found that, in 1976, Souter referred to abortion as "the killing of unborn children." He also said that affirmative action programs were "affirmative discrimination."

During a 1977 interview, Souter said a proposal to remove state restrictions on abortion would make New Hampshire "the abortion mill of the United States." These comments suggested that Souter was likely to side with the conservative justices of the Supreme Court—including Chief Justice William Rehnquist. But no one could be sure until Souter became a Supreme Court Justice and faced the issues.

In September 1990, David Souter faced the Senate Judiciary Committee for his confirmation hearings. After one week of questioning, Souter revealed little about his personal views.

Souter did reply about *Roe vs. Wade.* "I have not made up my mind," he said. "And I would not go on the Court saying I must go one way or I must go the other way." He then stated that he would keep an open mind about each case.

Souter was under no legal obligation to discuss his personal views. The Senate wasn't even supposed to be asking him such questions. The goal was to find out if Souter was qualified to be a Supreme Court Justice. No one could argue that he wasn't qualified. Souter was eventually approved by the Judiciary Committee. All he needed now was approval by the full Senate.

While awaiting final confirmation, David Souter returned to New Hampshire and received a hero's welcome. He visited friends. He caught up on his sleep. And he began answering the 900 letters he had received. Once while Souter was grocery shopping, admirers crowded around him for 90 minutes. In October 1990, David Souter learned he had been confirmed by the Senate.

"Could You Get the Door, Dave?"

Since David Souter was the newest Supreme Court Justice, he was considered the "rookie." As the rookie, he was given a few additional tasks that the veteran justices didn't care to do.

Souter answered the door at the justices' private Friday meetings in the Supreme Court Building in Washington, D.C. He took notes and reviewed the meeting with the court clerks afterward. And he was given the dullest opinions to write.

As the rookie, Souter also got last choice of office space. A secretary and a messenger were assigned to him. But his locker was in the robing room just behind the velvet curtains of the court chamber. Souter also received a customized chair for the bench.

Souter takes the oath of office as a Supreme Court Judge as Erin Rath, the daughter of a family friend, holds a Bible. Chief Justice Rehnquist administered the oath as President George Bush looks on.

Souter got a tour of the legal library and the gym. Then he went to work, pouring over case after case that had been piling up before the Supreme Court's current nine-month term.

So what role would David Souter play as an associate justice? It was still too early to tell. But there was little doubt that Souter would have an impact. With the recent resignations of some of the more liberal justices, many felt that the Supreme Court was at a crossroads—and that change would occur.

"When you get a new justice," Supreme Court Justice Sandra Day O'Connor said, it's more than a new justice. You get a new Court. In ways that are subtle and not so subtle, we change."

The Deciding Vote

Souter made his mark after only eight months on the Supreme Court. He provided the deciding vote in three controversial cases. In *Arizona vs. Fulminante*, Souter agreed with the majority that confessions obtained forcibly from criminals may be permitted in court. In *Auto Workers vs. Johnson Controls*, Souter agreed that barring women of childbearing years from hazardous jobs was against anti-discrimination laws.

Souter's most controversial opinion came in *Rust vs. Sullivan*. In this case, Souter and the majority of his fellow justices agreed that doctors in government-funded clinics could not counsel patients about abortion.

Souter's decision outraged those who favored abortion rights. They claimed the ruling violated a woman's right to an abortion, and a doctor's First Amendment right to speak.

But in the written opinion, the Court said: "The government has not discriminated on the basis of viewpoint. It has merely chosen to fund one activity (abortion) to the exclusion of another (counseling)."

The issue bitterly divided the Supreme Court. "The purpose and result of the challenged regulations is to deny women the ability voluntarily to decide their procreative destiny," said Justice Harry Blackmun in his written dissent.

It now appeared that David Souter's view on abortion was coming to light. Many feared he would eventually help overturn the law that granted women the right to an abortion. That, however, remains to be seen.

A protestor voices her opinion on the contoversial abortion issue.

The members of the Supreme Court pose for their 1990 photo. Shown are, bottom row (L to R) Associate Justices Harry Blackmun and Byron White, Chief Justice

William Rehnquist, Associate Justices Thurgood Marshall and John Paul Stevens. Top row (L to R) Anthony Kennedy, Sandra Day O'Connor, Antonin Scalia, and David Souter.

The Private Side of David Souter

Supreme Court Justices often take a low profile when it comes to their private lives. David Souter has always been a private man and little is known about his personal life.

Souter is a frugal man. He lives in a modest house in Weare, New Hampshire. His neighbors say he is quiet. He rarely answers the telephone at night. Not surprisingly, Souter enjoys reading, and maintains an extensive home library.

The home of David Souter in Weare, New Hampshire, where he has lived since he was 11 years old.

Souter is also a religious man. He attends service at a nearby Episcopalian Church on a regular basis. On the rare occasion that he drinks, Souter makes sure there is plenty of water in his liquor. Souter also watches his diet.

He often eats cottage cheese for lunch.

Souter is still a bachelor (he's never been married). When he arrived in Washington, D.C., Souter was placed at the top of every matchmaker's most eligible list. But Souter works long hours and rarely dates.
The women who know him say that Souter is "very warm, friendly, and a real gentleman." But his true love is the law.

"I think he gets lonely sometimes," said one of Souter's friends. "I think his work has been a tremendous release in that regard."

Supreme Court Justice David Souter will strengthen the Supreme Court's shift to the right.

The Silent Justice

So far, David Souter has remained a silent justice. As of May 1991, he had written only two opinions out of more than 60 that have been authored since he joined the Court.

Often when he concurs (agrees) with the majority opinion, Souter does not state his reasons. If he continues a conservative position, David Souter will strengthen the Supreme Court's shift to the right.

Glossary

Abortion: Expulsion of a human fetus during the first 12 weeks of gestation.

Congress: The lawmaking body of the United States of America.

Conservative: Inclined to keep things as they are or were in the past.

Constitution: The fundamental law of a state which guides and limits the use of power by the government.

Controversy: A discussion marked by the expression of opposing views: Dispute.

Justice: The determination of rights according to the rules of law.

Law: A rule of conduct or action prescribed or formally recognized as binding or enforced by a ruling authority.

Legislature: The branch of government that is charged with such powers as making laws.

Liberal: A person favorable to progress or reform.

Senate: A governing or lawmaking assembly. The Congress of the United States is the Senate and the House of Representatives.

Sophisticated: Highly complicated or developed.

United States Court of Appeals: A court hearing appeals.

Index